COSMIC!

DEVON VOL I

Edited by Carl Golder

GW00808659

First published in Great Britain in 1998 by
POETRY NOW YOUNG WRITERS
1-2 Wainman Road, Woodston,
Peterborough, PE2 7BU
Telephone (01733) 230748

HB ISBN 0 75430 207 5
SB ISBN 0 75430 208 3

FOREWORD

With over 63,000 entries for this year's Cosmic competition, it has proved to be our most demanding editing year to date.

We were, however, helped immensely by the fantastic standard of entries we received, and, on behalf of the Young Writers team, thank you.

Cosmic Devon Vol I is a tremendous reflection on the writing abilities of 8 & 9 year old children, and the teachers who have encouraged them must take a great deal of credit.

We hope that you enjoy reading *Cosmic Devon Vol I* and that you are impressed with the variety of poems and style with which they are written, giving an insight into the minds of young children and what they think about the world today.

CONTENTS

William O'Sullivan	79
Bethan Lewis	80
Isabel Ehresmann	81
Jason Hunt	82
Jamie Houlston	83
Jamie Fleming	83
Caragh Campbell	84
Laura Smith	85
Finbar Roth	86
Emma Waterworth	86
Christopher Merrett	87
Dominic Pain	87
Ruby Grantham	88
Yann Frampton	89
Jack Honeysett	90
Scott Mills	90
Emily Pitts	91
Daniel Stenson	91
Kate Baker	92

The Dolphin School

Grace Whitton	92
Amanda Fowler	93
Victoria Launchbury	94
Kelly Miller	95
Tabitha Lucy Quilter	96
Ben Hutchings	97
Alice Bowring	98
Mark Massarik	99

Uplowman Primary School

Kylie Rowe	100
Celia Hodgson	100
Colin Nicholls	101
Tim Sheridan	101
Kieran Knowles	102
Mark Ede	102
Simon Hawkins	103

Winkleigh CP School

THE POEMS

ANGEL FISH

Angel fish, angel fish
Down into the deep.
Lives the Queen of the
Angel fish.
She is pink, red and
orange too.
Her tail's like a silk sheet
in the shade of maroon.
And you cannot find an
Angel fish as lovely as she.

Jemma Cassar (9)
All Saints (Marsh) Primary School

BUBBLES

Bubbles in the air
Bubbles floating in the air
Bubbles everywhere
Bubbles popping.

Arron Johnson (8)
All Saints (Marsh) Primary School

BUBBLES

Bubbles sailing through the air
Green, peach, pink and blue
Different colours all for you
Down down to the ground
Pop!

Rebecca Hopkins (8)
All Saints (Marsh) Primary School

BUBBLES

Bubbles shiny in the light
For my great delight
Blue red and green too
Shininess in the night
I like it when they twist
They twist and twist
And twist until they pop.

Sophie Crews (8)
All Saints (Marsh) Primary School

BUBBLES

Bubbles
blown up through
the air
skimmed like an aeroplane,
Popping in the waste
paper bin.
Colours of the rainbow.

Jude Patrick Medcalf (8)
All Saints (Marsh) Primary School

BUBBLES

Floating bubbles bounce up and down
Everything they touch, they go pop
All the colours start to go.

Samantha Deamer (8)
All Saints (Marsh) Primary School

JUDO GRADING

First came the early start
That is the worst part
Then I got dressed
And made a mess
Which I now regret
Then I got my licence out
At half-past eight about
Then I got in the car
And the hall wasn't far
Then I started my fight
And fought and fought
As much as I could
But then I was down in a pin
All the rest seemed like a dream
I lost all my fights
But still got a stripe!

Natasha Ross (8)
All Saints (Marsh) Primary School

BUBBLES

Bubbles bubbles in the air
Bubbles bubbles everywhere
Purple, orange, green and blue
You won't know what to do
They're bouncing, skimming
Twirling around
Hurry up come and see them
Before they pop on the ground.

Danielle Tozer (8)
All Saints (Marsh) Primary School

BUBBLES

Bubbles with all those colours green, yellow
The colours in the world.
Bubbles when I blow pop where do they go?
Bubbles all of them like doubles
Why don't they stop *pop!*
Bubbles it looks like Mystic Meg's ball
Bubbles bubbles all the colours in the world
Yellow, red, blue, green, orange, pink, purple, gold,
silver, bronze, burgundy
Bubbles on me. Bubbles that tell the future
It sounds like it looks like Mystic Meg's ball
Bubbles floating in the air and shaped like a pear.

Alex Shuffell (7)
All Saints (Marsh) Primary School

IN THE HOSPITAL

My tongue is mute
The words are locked
Inside my head, beside my bed
A bowl of fruit and you who
Smile and talk to me
And hold my hand
And I smile
And I go to sleep
When they took me down
To the theatre and
I come from the theatre
But I cannot speak.

Wesley Westaway (9)
All Saints (Marsh) Primary School

BUBBLES

Bubbles float
Low and high
Bubbles go side to side
They go in circles
There are bubbles in the air
Bubbles everywhere
They twist and turn
And go over fields
My big bubble says goodbye
Remember bubbles are everywhere
My big bubble is a friend to everyone
He likes adventures
His name is Mgee
When he pops it means he's asleep
Mgee is see-through but
Mgee does not say goodbye
But pop goodbye.

Shawna Brady-Lavis (8)
All Saints (Marsh) Primary School

BUBBLES

Bibdy bibdy bop the bubbles go
pop like blue and green
up and down
Bibdy, bibdy pop!

Christopher Stubbs (8)
All Saints (Marsh) Primary School

DOGS

Dogs are small
Dogs are tall
There's the Cocker Spaniel
And the Springer Spaniel
In the cellar
You would find a Rottweiller
And a Doberman Pincher
Standing on guard
And police dogs smelling lard
Bloodhounds are
Good at smelling bombs
And you will find
The sausage dog is very long.

Tamsin Allen (8)
All Saints (Marsh) Primary School

SNOW AND ICE

Snow can be fun
Snow can be dangerous
Listen to this poem then you'll learn.
Ice we skate on, it's cool
Snow is round, ice is flat
Snow is soft, ice is hard.
Snow is like ice crystals, we can skate on ice
Ice can melt, snow can melt
Snow is round and soft.

Kirsty Brown (8)
All Saints (Marsh) Primary School

ON A SUNNY DAY

On a sunny day,
I go out to play.
In the paddling pool
I stay,
In the garden,
On a sunny day
With my toys I play.
Now it is not a sunny day,
And I do not want to play.

Katie Cane (9)
All Saints (Marsh) Primary School

DOGS

Dogs are big
Dogs are small
Dogs can be bad
Dogs can be fun
But there's a good pet
For everyone.

Emily Bunday (9)
All Saints (Marsh) Primary School

MY PUPPY ELVIS

My puppy Elvis has walked a mile.
My puppy Elvis wags his tail.
My puppy Elvis sits on a stile.
My puppy Elvis always howls.

Hannah Fowell (8)
All Saints (Marsh) Primary School

I WANT TO BE A PET!

I want to be a pet
So I can see a vet
The vet will say 'Hi'
My mum would almost cry
Because she thinks I will die
Then my mum will really cry
Then says 'Bye'
And I will ask 'Why'
'Because You might die.'

Laura Priscott (9)
All Saints (Marsh) Primary School

WOODS WALK

The woods are dark
in the night.
The owls hunt in the moonlight.
In the morning birds will sing.
The sunlight yawning in the morning.
I wake up early and play with the squirrels,
In the woods one spring day.

Jade Bolt (9)
All Saints (Marsh) Primary School

SPACE

Space is a basket for all the planets
Space is a big room with no light
Space is a big country with no boundaries
Space is a big bus for all the asteroids
Space is a rocket travelling through outer space.

Christopher Avery (9)
All Saints (Marsh) Primary School

I WANT TO BE A VET!

I want to be a vet
Then I could have a pet
I could have a dog or a hog
But I don't want a frog
I could have a cat and a rat
But I don't want a bat
I could have a mouse but not loose in my house
I could have anything I want
If I was a vet.

Abaigeal Gould (8)
All Saints (Marsh) Primary School

THE SKATEBOARD QUEEN

Here she comes
Sally the queen
Skating and sliding
Like the skating queen
All she does is
Skate, skate, skate
All day long with her
Mate, mate, mate.

Gemma Finnemore (8)
All Saints (Marsh) Primary School

STARS

Stars sparkle like ice melting
Stars pretty in the sky
Stars moving everywhere
And stars going round and round.

Rebecca Docking (9)
Bassetts Farm CP School

BRIGHT STARS

When I look up into space,
I could see sparkling stars
and milky chocolate bars.
Bright star whizzing through
the sparkling sky
Going through the windy wind
Space space, stars are really pretty.

Amy-Rose Kennedy (8)
Bassetts Farm CP School

SPACE

Earth is our planet
Whirling around the sun
Our star
Nine planets making the solar system
Out of a huge dark cloud
Of gas and dust.

Thomas Wakefield (7)
Bassetts Farm CP School

SPACE

In space I see
Stars
Spacemen
Spaceships
Moon
Planets
Space station.

Sam Ronayne (9)
Bassetts Farm CP School

STARS

Stars swim in the sky like giant sparks,
Giving off as much light as they can,
Shooting stars are different,
They shoot across the sky faster than a rocket,
Search for them before they hit another star,
Whoops! There goes another one,
Stars die just like humans,
They explode like dynamite,
A star could be dying now.

Josh Heyde (8)
Bassetts Farm CP School

SPACE

I would love to be up high,
Floating by stars and planets,
Will I get there tonight,
I wonder if I'll ever see the stars shining bright,
Unless they fall out of the night.

Joanna Smith (9)
Bassetts Farm CP School

THE MOON

When I was on the moon
it was cold, dark and scary.
I was speechless.
All around I saw big stars
and planets too.

Laura Myers (7)
Bassetts Farm CP School

SPACE

When I go out to space I will see
a moon and some stars
floating around.
In the sky it will be dark,
out into space aliens will be
floating around.
The moon is made of cheese.

Jamie Dawe (8)
Bassetts Farm CP School

THE MOON

The moon is just a big potato
Floating in the sky.
Little men from outer space are often passing by.
When they're feeling hungry
They might eat a bit for dinner,
That's why the moon is sometimes fat
And other times it's thinner.

Samuel Prosser (8)
Bassetts Farm CP School

PLANETS

Mercury's like a boiling oven,
Asteroids are big lumps of ice-cream,
Jupiter is like a big round football,
Mars is like a Frisbee in the sky,
All swirling round the sun.

Tim Bradshaw (8)
Bassetts Farm CP School

STARS UP IN SPACE

When I look at the stars
they twinkle
I see shooting stars
and I see satellites.
If you go up into space you
see shooting stars
and you might see
an alien on the moon.

Charlie Hanson (9)
Bassetts Farm CP School

SWEET SPACE

When I look up to the sky I think
when it's dark I could go up there and
feast on the gigantic Galaxy and the lovely Milky Way.
I could stay up there and I would never get hungry.
But when will it be? When could I really eat the Galaxy?

Emma Sear (8)
Bassetts Farm CP School

SPACE

Space has aliens
Space is dark
Space is round and big
Space has got stars
Space is a place you have never been to.
Space is quiet.

Sara Donald (7)
Bassetts Farm CP School

STARS, STARS

Stars, stars, up above in the sky.
I can see you with my eyes
I am coming up to get you
I swim in the sky but now I fall,
Fall down below the ground.
Stars up above I wish I could
Touch you, but you're too bright.

Chantelle Blinco (7)
Bassetts Farm CP School

SPARKLING STAR

Sparkling star in the sky all alone
No one to play with,
Sparkling star needs a friend.
I can see you sparkling in the sky and
I wish I could be your friend, twinkling star.

Catherine Duck (8)
Bassetts Farm CP School

SPACE

Space is dark,
Space is bright,
Space is a huge, hairy monster,
Space is creepy,
Space has aliens with big hairy kisses.

Rachel Maker (8)
Bassetts Farm CP School

STARS

Stars are yellow,
Stars are bright.
They show up at night,
When you look they are bright
Stars are yellow, stars are bright
In the sky there are lots of stars.
Stars are shining in the sky
Shining down on the Earth below
Stars cover the sky.
All I can see is stars,
Stars, more stars.
Stars are whizzing through the sky,
Stars are in space.

Holly Pinney (8)
Bassetts Farm CP School

I FEEL THINGS

I feel starfish swimming round my feet,
And feel birds flying in the sky,
I feel parrots speaking to me,
And stars whizzing in the sky,
I see kittens sitting by the fire,
And people singing loud,
I feel bears shouting,
And hear the lake laughing,
I see space in the sky.

Ashley Morrow (8)
Bassetts Farm CP School

THE PLANETS

Mercury, like a boiling oven,
Venus is the meanest,
Earth, where I live,
Mars, the red planet
Asteroids, huge lumps of ice-cream,
Jupiter a big orange and red planet,
Saturn, the king of the rings,
Uranus, a beautiful jewel,
Neptune, the greeny-bluey planet
Pluto, the icy cold planet.

Luke Webber (9)
Bassetts Farm CP School

STARS IN THE NIGHT

Pretty stars shine so bright
The prettiest star I ever saw
Shines so bright in the night,
I wonder if I'm going to the sky
Up there tonight I see the biggest stars.
I hope I fly up there tonight.
Pretty stars in the sky
Come down here
And say goodnight.

Lisa Donald (7)
Bassetts Farm CP School

STAR

Star bright
Star shining in the night
Star yellow
Star gold
Star shining in the night.

Lauren Croasdale (8)
Bassetts Farm CP School

MY FAMILY

My family is all right.
I like to play football.
I run with all my might
but I always seem to fall.

My name is Nickie M.
I like playing on the PC.
My next-door neighbour,
She's called Em.
We play on it after tea.

I like football
but *I hate school.*
Here are some of the things
I like best of all.
Spice Girls, Newcastle.

Nickie Morgan (7)
Broadwoodwidger CP School

MY BATH

This is my bath today.
I watch the water run away.
I like to swirl the flannel round
and listen to the songs and sounds.
My soap makes bubbles
big
and
small.
I blow them all.
Then I swiggle when I dry.
Mum says 'Bedtime.'
So then I cry!

Paul Marshall (8)
Broadwoodwidger CP School

IF I WAS

If I was a hungry rat,
and wanted something nice to eat.
I'd look in the fridge
and nibble something sweet.
I would eat up all the food.
Cheese, chocolate and strawberry jelly.
I wouldn't stop eating
until all the food was in my belly.

James Whitlock (7)
Broadwoodwidger CP School

POOR OLD DAD

Poor old dad,
His car's all bent.
It's all smashed up
A sad event.
We're very sorry,
It's done this now.
It must have been wrecked
By the cow.

Jonathan Hopper (9)
Broadwoodwidger CP School

A LIMERICK

There was a young boy
called Sam.
He liked jumping in jam.
So he went to the bath tub
and had a good scrub.
So Sam got rid of the jam.

Alex Tithecott (7)
Broadwoodwidger CP School

MY FAMILY

My brother is stupid,
My sister is too,
I'm really cool,
So are you.

My mum is naggy,
My dad is fun,
My grandad is strong,
Now my poem is done.

Ben Tainsh (8)
Broadwoodwidger CP School

SCHOOL

Run around the classroom,
terrifying teachers,
chasing with a broom,
smashing up their features.

Then in a late October,
to another school I went,
it was so boring, I couldn't stand it
so, to another I was sent.

Sammy Roberts (9)
Broadwoodwidger CP School

FLYING RIVER

Babbling at the beginning,
then swirling, diving, leaping.
Getting calmer as it widens
then tumbling down to a certain death,
crashing spray everywhere.
Quickly dashing, gurgling on and on.
Getting slower, widening, quietening,
at last it has reached the sea
but it's shy of meeting the waves
but it has to. *Ssshhh . . . Ssshhh.*
Lots of children come and play with it.
It is happy now.

Lauren Ashton (9)
Buckfastleigh Primary School

ORANGE SUNSET

Sunset bleeds into clouds,
And it always shouts aloud,
'I'm coming
I'm going'
With all the heat showing,
With the sun going down,
The evening sets still,
Over the town.

Lauren Goodwin (8)
Buckfastleigh Primary School

PIRATE ADVENTURE

When the foaming seas were salty,
And the pirate ship was sailing,
When the pirates themselves were drinking
and sang this very old song:
'Fifteen men on a dead man's chest,
Yo ho ho and a bottle of rum,
Drink and the devil have done for the rest,
Yo ho ho and a bottle of rum.

Crrrunch went the boat when they reached the island,
The pirates jumped right off,
The seas were scatty, so the pirates moved on,
But searched for the treasure in the hold.

Even when they'd had enough,
Still they didn't start.
When at last they came upon a chest,
They'd been waiting for.

The pirates were full of joy,
As they went back to the boat,
As they set sail for the seas,
The fate they had to see.

They sailed along loud and swiftly,
Until one gave a shout,
That the boat was going down,
Into the deep blue sea.

Slowly the boat went down,
As the pirates were to drown,
A whale gulped up the treasure,
While the pirates were meeting their doom.

Becky Rowe (8)
Buckfastleigh Primary School

Rabbit

Jump so high
We think you're a kangaroo.
Soft tail
So soft
We think it's snow.
Sharp claws
Can scratch you . . .
But we don't think you will.

Stephanie Abbott (6)
Buckfastleigh Primary School

Springtime

Springtime's yellow sun,
It makes me feel happy.
Children playing, having fun,
Under a bright yellow sun.
Yellow sand feels warm and gritty
Under my hands.

Aimee Rollings (9)
Buckfastleigh Primary School

Dinosaur

Jumps as high as a cloud
Runs as fast as an ostrich
Sharp teeth are like spikes
He'll eat you up
Roarrrrrr!

Daniel Partridge (6)
Buckfastleigh Primary School

SCARY CAT

I saw a hen in a pig pen.
I saw a hog eating a dog.
I saw a louse as large as a mouse,
Those are such strange things.

The cat was scared of the bat.
The bat was scared of the rat.
The rat was scared of the mat
I am scared of everything.

Clare Halls (7)
Buckfastleigh Primary School

LEARNING AND LAUGHING

One, two, three
Listen to me.
Four, five, six, seven and eight
Leave me alone to concentrate.

Lauren Ellis (7)
Buckfastleigh Primary School

FUNKY NUMBERS

One witty witch went to Wales.
Two ticklish tortoises toured the town.
Three thick thorns threw thistles.
Four pheasants flew over forests.
Five flies flicked flowers fluidly.

Kim Renshaw (9)
Decoy CP School

THE PENGUIN

Penguins waddle,
Swim in a puddle.
Catching fish in a dish.
Meeting penguins as he passes,
And sees one with glasses!
Their black and white feathers,
Smelling like heather.
You welcome little fishes in your dishes,
And gobble them up,
And then you see a seal pup!
Hurry up! Hurry up!
Otherwise you'll get gobbled up!

Lauren Taskis (8)
Decoy CP School

NINE NUTTY NAMES

My friend Sue always visits the zoo.
My friend Jim is very thin.
My friend Al is a very nice pal
My friend Molly loves her little dolly.
My friend Shane fell off a plane.
My friend Pete eats Shredded Wheat.
My friend Natalie has a nice family.
My friend Dale swims like a whale.
My brother Daniel looks like a cocker spaniel.

Kerry McBride (8)
Decoy CP School

A RECIPE FOR WINTER

Take some deep white snow.
Some cheering children sledging on the crisp steep hills,
and grandpas and grandmas poking their little blazing fires
as the smoke rises through the chimney.
Mix with parents going to work,
striding across the crackling frost on the grass.
Decorate it with some berries
and green prickly holly.
Then leave it in the freezer for three and a half months
and you have made winter!

Steven Fursdon (9)
Decoy CP School

CHRISTMAS

Crackers banging loudly in the kitchen.
Holly blowing in the strong wind.
Rudolf's nose shining brightly.
Ice melting on the ground.
Santa flying swiftly in the cloudy sky.
Tinsel sparkling on the tree.
Mice squeak to the sound of 'White Christmas.'
Apple pies ready to be eaten.
Sleigh bells ringing to the spirit of Christmas.

Lucy Trotman (9)
Decoy CP School

RECIPE FOR SUMMER

Take some deep golden sand,
some colourful flowers pink, purple, red
and yellow and pink blooms opening.

Add some bright blue sea,
some white baby sea horses
thrashing onto the golden sand
and coloured fishes deep, deep below the sea.

Mix with days of brilliant sunshine,
some beach balls striped red, blue, green, yellow and purple
and children sunbathing and paddling
in brightly coloured swimming costumes
with their mothers.

Decorate with birds singing
and children making sand castles
that soon get washed away at sunset.

Leave in the cooker for three long months,
and you have made summer.

Francesca Tuckerman (9)
Decoy CP School

BONFIRE NIGHT

Bright sparks in the dark,
Dancing above the bonfire,
Flames sparkle and dance.

Orange, red and green,
Dragon spitting flying flames
Raining sparks above.

Michael Cox (9)
Decoy CP School

A Cat's Day

Cats stretch in the morning,
With a good morning *'Miaow'*
They purr when they are happy,
Swish their tails when they are sad,
With a little wet nose,
And only four toes,
With cute little eyes that glow,
At night sometimes they go
For a midnight stroll,
With legs as strong as poles,
They lay down on the floor
Slowly shuffle forwards,
Jump up and catch a mouse or two,
Sometimes they bring mice to their owners as a present,
But never could they possibly bring a pheasant!

Emilie Maybury-Jenks (8)
Decoy CP School

Bonfire Haiku

Flames cover the Guy,
Orange cinders fill the sky,
Red hot glowing ash.

Fireworks like comets,
Fiery dragon spitting sparks,
Rain of ash shoots down.

Jonathan Widnall (9)
Decoy CP School

Ooops!

We were all in the back yard,
Singing a footie song,
We were about to play a soccer game,
The problem is they're all the same,
We picked the teams, they were unfair,
But nobody seemed to care,
The kick-off was taken,
I was going wrong somewhere,
Hang on, I'm running the wrong way,
I kicked the ball high in the air,
Ooops!
It went loopy loop,
And fell at my team mate's feet.
She chipped it towards me,
It landed on my head with a *thwack!*
It was only when it went in my own net,
I realised I'd headed it back.

Charlie Robinson (8)
Decoy CP School

Fireworks

Colourful sparks glow
Flickering flames fill the sky
Wood burns to ashes.

Noisy, loud fireworks
Glowing in the dark, black night
Bursting with colour.

Rachael Candy (9)
Decoy CP School

THE LION

The lion is a funny thing,
It's big and strong,
It weighs a ton,
Its browny mane is shabby.

It eats with its muddy paws.
It roars like a waterfall,
Its young are called cubs,
They do not have pubs,
Nor do they have rugs,
They sleep bare,
They have lots of hair,
They are very rare,
So that's the lion.

Edward Glover (8)
Decoy CP School

SUPER TORTOISE

Is it a plane?
Is it a bird?
Is it a cat with wings?
No, It's Super Tortoise.

He flies through the air with the greatest of ease,
Look at that tortoise with no flying trapeze.

He hasn't been beaten yet
He is as strong as a gladiator
He's faster than a plane
And he lives in my garden.

Tom Utley (9)
Decoy CP School

THE METAL HORSE

The metal horse does canter by
His metal hinges creak and sway
The metal saddle bumps up and down
On his rickety back.
He changes his canter from trot to walk
He stops and stares
His big black eyes do glitter
And out of the darkness a fox appears.
Which scares the metal horse
We do not know where he came from
All we know is that he is real
And we know he runs like the wind.

Verity C Walker (9)
Decoy CP School

THE LIFE OF A BIRTHDAY CANDLE

The candle flickers
in the dark, dark nights.
We blow the candle
out in the day.
The candle melts and
slowly shrinks.
It jumps
when the wind rushes by.
It gives us memories from
long ago, and it gives
us birthday wishes.

William Jennings (8)
Decoy CP School

MY CANDLE

Candles glow all night and day,
Sitting in a lump of clay,
Flame growing higher and higher,
Orange glowing, little fire.
Candles glow all night and day,
Over the hills and far away.
Filtering reflection on the table,
Sitting there nice and stable.
Candles glow all night and day,
Let's just hope it doesn't lay.
Melting down really fast,
Let's just hope the candle lasts.

Lynne Gilbrook (9)
Decoy CP School

BADGER, BADGER!

Badger, badger over there,
You have got a lot of hair.
On your nose and on your tail,
Slide along a slippery trail.

Your nose is black and white,
You are a beautiful sight.
You are as white as white,
As black as black and as grey as grey,
As you nuzzle in the hay.

Alexandra Heath (8)
Decoy CP School

THE CANDLE LIGHT

Candles dancing round and round
Lovely colours all around
Tall flame burning all day long
Different colours bobbing along
Little flame, big flame dancing round
The flame starts to burn to the ground.
A small tear forms in my eye
As the candle starts to die.
My birthday's nearly over
And the candle's nearly gone
It will not survive another year
Goodbye, candle, goodbye.

Elaine Avery (9)
Decoy CP School

THE GOLDFISH POEM

Bubble, bubble, bubble
Who's swimming in the tank?
It is Mrs Goldfish,
She is eating her fish flakes
Swimming in some water,
Floating when they swim,
Eating fishy chocolates,
Swimming by the weed.

Rachel Billing (8)
Decoy CP School

CANDLE, CANDLE, CANDLE

The candle's been lit, lit, lit
It's going to spit, spit, spit.
It's bright with a flickering light,
It's melting away
It won't last all day.
The candle glows
As it shows
Its yellow flame flickering
Like a teardrop from my eye.
When I blow
There is no glow
Because the candle's died.

Jamie Stevens (9)
Decoy CP School

CANDLES GLOWING

Candles glow all night and day.
Sitting in a lump of clay.
Flame growing higher and higher.
Orange glowing little fire.

Candles glow all night and day.
Over the hills and far away.
Flickering reflection on the table,
Sitting there nice and stable.

Chris Crossley (8)
Decoy CP School

ABC ALPHABET

A
B oy had a
C olourful
D uck. It looked
E normous. It sounded very
F ierce. Every morning it would
G rumble and quack
H appily.

Samuel Pickett (8)
Decoy CP School

MY DOGGY TODDY

My dog is black and white,
Sleeps all day and plays all night,
Running around the garden,
Squeezing through the fence,
One thing is for certain, he makes my
Dad so tense.

Jonathan Lewis (9)
Decoy CP School

BONFIRE NIGHT

Fireworks sparkling high.
Fireworks shooting at the moon
Zooming into the night.

Bonfires burning.
Bonfire flames burn up Guy.
Bonfire flames burn.

Paul Preece (9)
Decoy CP School

BIRTHDAY CANDLE

Candles glow all night and day,
Sitting on a lump of clay,
Flame glowing higher and higher,
Orange glowing little fire.

Candles glow all night and day,
Over the hills and far away,
Flickering reflection on the table,
Sitting there nice and stable.

Candles glow all night and day,
Let's just hope it doesn't lay,
Melting down really fast,
Let's just hope that candle lasts.

Kayleigh Wyatt & Lynne Gilbrook (9)
Decoy CP School

A RECIPE OF SUMMER

Take some deep golden sand,
Some seagulls squawking in the deep blue sky.
Add some bright blue sea
Some great pale clouds
And a glistening sun in the sky.
Mix with days of brilliant sunshine,
And the sky shining brightly,
And children playing in the brilliant sunshine.
Leave in the cooker for
Three long months,
And you have made summer.

James Rumbelow (9)
Decoy CP School

THE LIFE OF A BIRTHDAY CANDLE

A candle is bright,
With a glowing light,
It sways and melts,
in the blowing breeze,
The flame is light,
It is like the heat
Of the sun.
It melts into
The pink flower holder,
Then I blow out
The candle,
And make a wish.

Lauren Ford (8)
Decoy CP School

SOUNDS

The tinkle winkle of the tin
the chatter batter of the cutlery
the clang bang of the bell.

The whisper twisper of the chain
the bang ham lam of the hammer
the ping pang ding dang ping of the keys.

The rattle tattle of the train
the battle tattle rattle of the knife and fork
the lamber bamber tamber of the chain,
the tick tock of the mantel clock.

Melanie Rowland (9)
Decoy CP School

RECIPE FOR SPRING

Take some fresh, soft, smooth blossom,
Some stiff, brown bark
and a bit of bright blue sky.
Add some warm, prepared, yellow and
blue tulips,
Some bright red petals off a red
romantic rose,
and a deep white, dazzling daisy.
Mix with blue and pink wild flowers,
Some bright green, glistening leaves
and a spoonful of fresh, spring air.
Decorate with colourful, easy to
catch, butterflies,
some happy and cheerful spring days
sprinkled on top,
and some blue tits singing softly.
Leave it in the flower bed for three
whole months
and you have made spring.

Clara Milstead (9)
Decoy CP School

SNAIL TRAIL

A snail leaves a silver trail,
On the lawn and on the wall
On bushes big and small.

The snail's protection is its shell,
It eats flowers and grass as well.

That's why gardeners hate the snail,
With its glimmering silver trail.

Edward Lewis (9)
Decoy CP School

METAL SOUNDS

The ting of a bell,
The tinkle of a tin,
The ping of keys,
The chime of a metal dustbin.

The clank of a chain,
The clatter of cutlery,
The rattle of trains,
The banging of a hammer on a nail.

The scraping of a knife and fork,
The popping of a metal cork,
The creak of an iron hinge,
All those sounds I know so well.

Thomas Petas (9)
Decoy CP School

SLUGS AND SNAILS

Slugs and snails leave sparkling trails,
On the garden wall.
They're little squashy things,
They have not got any intelligence at all.
They can't swim in the swimming pool,
They certainly do not go to school.
If you want them as a pet,
You *don't* take them to the *vet!*
Slugs and snails leave sparkling trails.

Jessica Neno (8)
Decoy CP School

A RECIPE FOR SUMMER

Take some deep golden sand
Some lollies dripping quickly
and some seagulls diving into the sea.
Add some bright blue sea
some sand in the bay
and some suntan lotion bright
and creamy.
Mix with days of brilliant sunshine
Some ice-cream licked by playful children
and some balls bouncing lightly.
Decorate with golden sun
Some sand tickling my shiny skin
and lots of sea swishing.
Leave in the cooker for three long
months, and you have made *summer!*

Meggie Pearce (9)
Decoy CP School

A RECIPE FOR WINTER

Take some deep white snow,
some cold trees
and church bells singing their
early song.

Add some red holly berries,
some crispy crunchy grass
and icy hard frozen ponds.

Mix with days of silver frost,
some furry, white cold scarves
and black gloves.

Decorate with warm fluffy hats
and coats.
Some drainpipes with icicles
hanging down.

David Robinson (9)
Decoy CP School

A RECIPE FOR SUMMER

Take some deep golden sand,
Some blue sea waving as the sun starts
going down,
and bright yellow sandcastles.
Add some bright blue sea,
Some seagulls flying in the sky,
and the green grass blowing in the breeze.
Mix with days of brilliant sunshine
Some flowers dancing in the fields
and barbecues which you can smell
in the gardens.
Decorate with birds singing in the tops of
green trees.
Some people dancing and singing on a
summer beach
and people sunbathing in the burning sand.
Leave in the cooker for three long months
and you have made summer all bright.

Lisa Wilson (9)
Decoy CP School

CHRISTMAS POEM

Crackers banging fiercely in people's hands.
Holly decorating up high with berries
as red as blood.
Rudolf riding in the starry sky.
Ice on the white window.
Sleigh bells ringing in the snow.
Twinkling tinsel up above us all.
Mistletoe hanging from the wall.
Angels on the green Christmas tree.
Stocking full of surprises.

Hayley Grove (9)
Decoy CP School

THE MOON AND STARS

The silver moon is shining down.
Shining on the earth below.
The stars are twinkling in the sky.
I wish I could go to see that place.

Ravisha Patel (7)
Grenville College Junior School

SPACE

Stars are twinkling in the sky
Shining their way to day
I feel glad when I see the moon shine on me.
I wish I was there too.

Peter Hockridge (8)
Grenville College Junior School

THE STARS

The twinkling stars above the world
Make a silver sky
Then the moon comes out to play
In the silvery sky
The twinkling stars above the world
Are up so high.

The twinkling stars above the world
Are so shy
They make different patterns every night
With so much light
The twinkling stars above the world
Shine upon me.

Matthew Cawsey (8)
Grenville College Junior School

THE SPRAYING ALIEN

Stars are shining glittering up above
In the pitch-black sky,
Far away up in space,
Quiet not a sound.
Up in space I can't see or smell
But I can hear big footsteps banging
Water spraying on me.
I start screaming,
Oh no!
It's an alien.

Joanna Williams (8)
Grenville College Junior School

THE UNIVERSE

The universe is wide and deep.
Who knows how many secrets it does keep
Pluto, Jupiter and Mars
And many undiscovered stars
Here on Earth we lie at night
Watching shooting stars burn bright
Rocket ships propel us high
Into the never ending sky
We see the sun each summer's day
Its rays shoot down to light our way
Man has walked upon the moon
And perhaps on Mars one day soon.

Christopher Deakes (8)
Grenville College Junior School

SPACE

Blasting off into space in an ex-mobile.
I love to watch the shooting stars
As they twinkle on the planet Mars.
It's such a quiet place to be.
I wish I could be here every day
Watching the aliens cobble their shoes.
I'm so lucky to be here,
It's not every day you come so near.

Hannah Standford (8)
Grenville College Junior School

COSMIC

I was in space at the age of the human race,
I was in a spaceship when I met an alien
without an upper lip,
Of course I was in Cosmic!
I crashed on Mars,
The strange thing was the aliens had cars.
Then I went to Saturn
The rings had been fattened,
There were millions of them,
All orange and lemon, and they looked
like a Mexican's hat.
Then on we went to Pluto,
Where the aliens played the fluto.
We took a left turn,
Crashed into the Plough!
Oh no! What shall we do now?
When we got to Mercury guess what was there
A turkey!
I've had enough of all of this
I must go home to see the things I miss.

Joe Morgan (8)
Grenville College Junior School

COSMIC

There's a world of spaceships,
Planets and stars out there.
It is a world of flashes and colours.
No one knows how it was formed in the world.
It is big and black and beautiful.

James Borrowdale (8)
Grenville College Junior School

SPACE

I think there's a monster after me
I'll look around the galaxy
There's many planets all shapes and sizes
Jupiter, the biggest, hot and sticky
Saturn with its rings and moons
Uranus and Neptune, similar to view
With a bluish tinge which changes their
Colour in the winds.
Earth is the next, my beloved planet
If only I could be back with my family and friends.
Venus, another with its dense thick cloud
And its hot and sticky surface.
Mercury is close to the sun but is difficult
To see with the naked eye.
Pluto the smallest of the planets I think
Cold and sparse, a lonely place.
Mars, I've missed its bright red colour
Covered in rock and dust, a rusty picture
I see in my mind.
Ice caps that melt in a period of time
Shadows, I fear are my monster friend,
Racing me to my destination.
Earth's next door neighbour is the moon
The place I want to be where so
Many astronauts have made a landing
But the one thing which is missing
Is the sea.

Amelia Bull (9)
Grenville College Junior School

THE UNIVERSE

I went to the moon
It was like a huge balloon
At night I looked up
Stars were all around me
And you could see the round planets shining
The morning soon came up, I moved a little bit on
I saw all green things coming up to me
They were aliens with eyes that dangle down
They told me to eat some cheese off the moon
I tried, it was very sour
But the aliens soon made friends in half an hour.

Alexandra Shortridge (9)
Grenville College Junior School

SILLY SPACEMAN

There was a spaceman, he went to space,
And he said 'This will be one large step for the human race.'
He went to pongy Pluto and silly Saturn
Suddenly he crashed
And the spaceship smashed.
Then he was stranded in space.
And he said 'I've made it to the end of the human race!'
Then he saw a light
And the poet didn't know what to write
So he jumped up high
And said 'I'm going to die'
But he couldn't get down from the sky.

Matthew Short (9)
Grenville College Junior School

THE EXCLAMATION MARK!

The *exclamation mark* is good for shouting.
It's always there after *stop!*
It's always after a caution sign.
The *exclamation mark!*

I wonder where it goes at night,
Out of my sight.
It's probably being used by another soul.

The *exclamation mark* is useful
When you are shouting -
It's always there when you need it.

Daniel Singh (9)
Grenville College Junior School

WILL IT BE SCARY, WILL IT BE NICE?

I wish I could go to the moon,
I'll come back to the Earth soon.
I wonder what it would be like
Would it be scary or would it be nice?
My brother would like to go to the galaxy
He wonders what will it be like
Will it be scary, will it be nice?
Well one day my mum took us there
But I would not like to live there.

Emma Westlake (9)
Grenville College Junior School

THE SPACE BOY

Look at the stars
High up in the sky
As we go by
Look at the moon
It's glittering and shining like
The stars
I like space, it's a very big place.

Christopher Teague (8)
Grenville College Junior School

SPACE

Space is the place
Where the moon and stars live
Space is the place to go
The sky sparkling bright with
stars so white
Space is a very big place
I wish I could be there.

Robert Reid (7)
Grenville College Junior School

SPACE

I'm in space on the place
The stars are gleaming in my face
I'm going round and round the moon.
The shooting stars are swishing all around me.
The stars are glittering in the sky.

Francesca Tomalin (7)
Grenville College Junior School

SHINING ON YOU

As I look up in the sky,
I see little things sparkling like diamonds.
I wonder why?
It would be nice if I could fly
Up in the sky.

Elizabeth Jury (8)
Grenville College Junior School

THE CLOCK

Tick tock, tick tock,
round and round,
The hands of the clock!

Tick, tock, tick, tock,
Slowing down,
Tick . . . tock!

They look at me,
They turn away,
Just hanging there all day!

I'm slowing down,
My batteries are failing,
No one can hear my crying and wailing!

My batteries stop,
My last tick tock,
But I can see, batteries coming to me.

They get popped in,
Then people can hear,
A brand new ticking sound,
Calling through their ear!

Nicola Augusti (9)
Rydon Primary School

SCARY MONSTERS

Sneaking up the stairs and along the landing
Creeping towards my bedroom door
Are monsters galore
Ravenous for human blood to drink.
Yes I can feel it, there's something behind
my bedroom door,
Making their way under the floorboards
On their way to tea.
No! They're coming through the floor
to drink my blood and eat my bones.
Stirring under the bed covers.
There's something leaning over me
Eerie creaks all about me
Right up close I hear it breathe
Stripping back the bed covers my mum
says 'Are you alright Dominic?'
It was a dream!

Dominic Moss (9)
Rydon Primary School

TEETH

My teeth are really healthy,
I brush them twice a day,
I don't eat sweets and all the sugar goes away.
But one day I went to the shop and bought a load of sweets
My teeth turned orange and dropped out by my feet.
I ran straight home to my mum and she sent me right upstairs.
I put all my teeth under my pillow, then I was a millionaire.

Robert Williams (9)
Rydon Primary School

BARNEY

Bark! Bark! Barney.
Are you lonely?
Running round the garden
Running round the roundabout
Why are you so lonely?
New collar, new lead,
You're such a spoilt dog.
Everywhere I looked,
Everywhere I looked,
At last I found my teddy book.
You're not lonely anymore,
You have your teddy book.
But I am so lonely.

Jessica Thompson (9)
Rydon Primary School

INDIANS

Indians fighting
All the time on cold green grass.
Night Indians!
Hello Indians!
Time for fighting now.
Goodbye Indians!
Indians eat meat.
Indians kill buffalo.
Indians cook fast!

Simon Titt (9)
Rydon Primary School

MY CATS

I have two black cats,
Gismo and Ben,
One of them is five,
The other is ten.
I love them to bits,
But sometimes I feed them too much.
One sleeps anywhere,
The other sleeps in a chair.
One of them goes and hides
Under a shed,
The other comes and sleeps by my bed.
I have two cats, Gismo and Ben,
One is five, the other is ten.

Hannah Pocock (9)
Rydon Primary School

FOOTBALL FAN

I'm a football fan
Just like my old man
We're both football crazy
But Mum says
We're just plain lazy.
But we don't agree
We just like to see
the Gunners on TV.

Stewart Noone (9)
Rydon Primary School

SCHOOL FRIENDS

I have many friends at school,
One day they like me the next day they don't,
So I'm sitting on a bench,
Watching them having fun,
I'm all sad just sitting there in a trance,
The end of play, I line up,
Next play I do the same again,
but all of a sudden they ask me to play?

Katie Cocks (9)
Rydon Primary School

FIVE LITTLE INDIANS

Five little Indians riding a pony.
Having fun for all eternity.
Lovely fresh air in the sky.
When they got home they put the pony
back in the stable.
The five little Indians happy with
their pony.

Kurt Collings (9)
Rydon Primary School

WILD HORSES

Wild horses racing through the canyon
All in a big stampede.
The cloud of dust behind them
Is really huge.
They must be running really fast.
All different colours.
Black, brown, white and spotted.
Wild horses are really nice.

Rebecca Winther (9)
Rydon Primary School

WINTER IS COMING

Winter is coming I can tell.
Snow is falling.
The car will not start.
Hedgehogs are hibernating.
We have to light the fire.
School is cancelled.
There are little boys outside in the
snow, they have made a snowman
and they are throwing snowballs.

Christopher Preston (9)
Rydon Primary School

APPROACHING THE RIVER

Tractors going like a stormy day,
Birds sing sweetly,
A helicopter brumming away,
The fields are full of horses and trees,
Now look, you can see the River Tavy,
It's as blue as the sky,
It's gleaming sparkling blue,
It's flowing so gracefully as if it was dancing,
We are getting closer and closer to the river,
Bit by bit it is getting louder,
Birds are twittering and woodpeckers are tapping
Just like a rap,
Whoosh! Whoosh!
There it goes,
As fast as a cheetah,
The noise is as loud as a
Lion!

Emma Bennett (9)
St Andrew's CE Primary School, Buckland Monachorum

TEETH

Shining teeth working away
Crushing molars grinding all day.
Powerful canines rip, munch and crunch
Without them you'd have no lunch!
Swiftly teeth chop up food
Cavities and decay make teeth quickly wear away.
Food out there, you'd better beware
                for teeth are on the loose!

Thomas Hall (9)
St Andrew's CE Primary School, Buckland Monachorum

IT'S TIME TO SAY GOODBYE

My mum passed me a photo
It was of her and Dad
I put it in my leather case,
It's time to say goodbye.

The lump in my throat
Grew bigger,
Each time I said goodbye to something,
Or someone,
I knew and loved.
It's time to say goodbye.

Goodbye bed, I say
As I pin my label on.
Goodbye sofa, goodbye chair
As my mum gives me my case.
It's time to say goodbye.

The train whistle blowing.
The white steam flowing
Like tears from our eyes.
The mothers crying heaving and sighing,
It's time to say goodbye.

Hannah Gardiner (9)
St Andrew's CE Primary School, Buckland Monachorum

MY MUM

Pretty Mum her hair is brown
Kind Mum she makes me omelettes every day
Working Mum she makes money for food
Loving Mum she never forgets me
Happy Mum she is always happy.

Keiren Biggs (7)
St Andrew's CE Primary School, Buckland Monachorum

APPROACHING THE RIVER

Birds tweeting as loud as dogs barking,
Noises coming from nowhere.
A red and green landscape, the red as red as fire.
Thorns and prickles everywhere,
Rivers whooshing anywhere,
Light green pastures,
Bright blue sky.
Woodpeckers pecking,
At grass-green trees.
People stepping,
Branches crunching,
Brambles getting tangled up,
Like people tying up a knot.
Noises here, noises there,
Noises everywhere.

Romin Pajouheshnia (9)
St Andrew's CE Primary School, Buckland Monachorum

FIREWORKS

In the fiery sky,
golden rain falls
like willow blossom.

Rockets like guns
firing green and blue bullets
up in the sky.

Catherine wheels
whizzing round and round
like the sparkling sun.

James Tailyour (7)
St Andrew's CE Primary School, Buckland Monachorum

APPROACHING THE RIVER

Birds sing like opera singers.
The crows fly like helicopters,
A woodpecker's tap is just like a rap,
Fields are green hankies.

The river rushes throughout the trees,
In and out the gorse,
If you listen carefully can you hear it?
Of course.

It rushes and gushes like a kettle boiling,
Swooping, soaring, flying is the buzzard,
Washing, raging over the rocks,
If you listen carefully, can you hear it?
Of course.

Rachel Greatrex (9)
St Andrew's CE Primary School, Buckland Monachorum

THE DREAM OF THE NAILS

I remember a long time ago
being put in flames,
being hammered into my shape,
being put in freezing cold water,
then I was made.

The young carpenter climbed on the cross.
Cruel men stuck me through His skin.
His blood spurted out.
I felt sorry for Him.
He had done nothing.

Edward Smith (8)
St Andrew's CE Primary School, Buckland Monachorum

CREEPY SHADOWS

I know I did
I know I did
I saw it Mum
I really did
I saw it creeping past our door.
It was big, black and creepy
Don't say that Mum
Help! I saw it just now.
It was looming about
I tried to touch
I got such a fright.
I couldn't touch it
Oh Mum, it was my friend.
It was her shadow
She said 'It was your own silhouette.'

Heidi Lowe (8)
St Andrew's CE Primary School, Buckland Monachorum

DRAGON!

Guarding his box of treasure,
beautiful, brassy, gold,
A dragon with smoking hot breath,
teeth like knives,
big webbed feet, green scary scales,
huge leathery wings,
golden sharp spikes,
a sweeping long tail
and a blue-gem eye
that opened and stared at me.

Christopher Smith (8)
St Andrew's CE Primary School, Buckland Monachorum

APPROACHING THE RIVER

Hearing the swallow, sweeping swallow
Screeching like a duck.
We think we hear a tractor
that sounds like a bulldozer yawning in
the night.
Hearing the grass whispering under your feet.
Hearing the helicopter like someone snoring
in the morning.
Hearing the river flowing gracefully along
like a swan flapping its wings.
and children playing in the sea with
dolphins swimming with mermaids.
Hearing the woodpecker pecking with a hammer
knocking a blue whale on the head.
Hearing the feet chattering on the path
while gold and silver fall on the grass
The waters rushing, rushing, rushing, down at the double
Water's where happiness and peace joins together.

Sophia Matthews (8)
St Andrew's CE Primary School, Buckland Monachorum

APPROACHING THE RIVER

Crows are croaking like a frog, *croak.*
Wind is singing softly, *la.*
Helicopters as loud as a windmill, *whoosh!*
Woodpeckers are like hammers, *bang!*
River like a whirlwind, *swoosh!*
Birds are like quiet bells, *tweet!*
Mice are like trees creaking, *eek!*
The sky is like the sea, *clear.*
       I hope you like it there.

Sammy Murphy (9)
St Andrew's CE Primary School, Buckland Monachorum

APPROACHING A RIVER

A helicopter rushing through the sky.
With the wind whooshing through the sky.
The birds tweeting with a loud voice.
A woodpecker pecking.
Grass and moss, soft and wet.
Smooth and comfortable.
The trees standing still in the wind.
All the sticks and brambles sticking up.
Huge big heavy stones in our way
River slithering all the way.
People whispering and whispering
As we walk across the sticks.
People are crunching, crunching,
Like if you are snapping a biscuit.

Claire Burrow (9)
St Andrew's CE Primary School, Buckland Monachorum

MOON DRAGON

I met a dragon flying over the moon.
His scales were like shining metal,
His eyes glowed in the dark.
His tail was like a hammer
hitting the stars.
Then he flew into orbit,
like a rocket breathing fire.
He vanished behind the moon
and left me behind.

Jenny Johnston (8)
St Andrew's CE Primary School, Buckland Monachorum

APPROACHING A RIVER

Birds sing where
Honeysuckle grows.
The sound stops
Where children arose.
A helicopter rings
Just like a train.
Woodpeckers tap and
Sound like a rap.
You feel like you're
Alone down in the snow.
Fields and hills touch
The sky.
The bright blue sky
Just like a blue planet
It catches your eye.
Shadows and trees
Come over wildlife.
Sounds of the river
I can finally hear.
Two rivers meet right into
One. Gushing and rushing
Down the river.

Jessica Parker (8)
St Andrew's CE Primary School, Buckland Monachorum

FIRE-BREATHER

Suddenly I saw the dragon.
He had hot fierce breath,
big fiery wings,
claws like knives,
a long spiky tail.

Megan Preece (8)
St Andrew's CE Primary School, Buckland Monachorum

MY MUM

Loving Mum loves me
Caring Mum cares for me
Kind Mum is very tidy.
She keeps the garden nice and smiley.
Busy Mum is round about
showing that she can shout.
Fit Mum has a walk
Long-haired Mum gets in the way.
Short-haired Mum does not
get in the way.
Funny Mum pushes me out the
other side of my bed,
Cross Mum is cross for a reason.
She loves you and me but she
doesn't want you to get shouted
at too much. She does love
you as much as me.

Mum loves me

Charlotte England (7)
St Andrew's CE Primary School, Buckland Monachorum

DRAGON

A dragon with a runny snout
kind blue eyes
with a hot fiery tongue.
Rich, kind dragon
and he had a kind heart
and soft feathery wings.

Kara Hook (8)
St Andrew's CE Primary School, Buckland Monachorum

APPROACHING THE RIVER

A woodpecker hammers on the trunk of a tree
Birds sing in the silence
A roar of an aeroplane breaks the sound
The gentle tinkle of the brook
And the chatter of excited children
The gentle sound of rushing water.

Greens and yellows with a gentle gold
Rustlings in the trees
Lawnmower humming
Fast footsteps on the grass
A bird twitters
A camera takes a photo with a whirr
The river is rushing to the sea.

Naomi Lear (9)
St Andrew's CE Primary School, Buckland Monachorum

TEETH

Bulky grinding powerful molars.
Stalagmites and stalactites waiting to tear and crush
in the cave-like mouth.
Tearing, biting canines ready to kill.
Burning, killing tooth decay.
Solid white enamel glinting.
Slimy saliva drips from the jaw.
Rounded jaws crunching together.

Elena Bridge (9)
St Andrew's CE Primary School, Buckland Monachorum

APPROACHING THE RIVER

Birds saying that spring has come,
Thrushes calling to their husbands.
Woodpeckers knocking like a pendulum,
But no sign of any gun.

Planes flying overhead,
Helicopters with whizzing rotor blades,
Invading the peace and quiet,
River flowing, stirring up mud from the bed,
Companions chattering like birds,
Bracken all around you,
Telegraph poles ruin the scene,
No more sounds of horses.

Now we've got to the river,
Admire the lovely banks,
Tuck into your lunch,
A bit more work for the liver.

David Jones (8)
St Andrew's CE Primary School, Buckland Monachorum

SHADOW POEM

Shadows creeping up on you in the dark
Spying on you.
Quickly hiding when you look round.
Never letting you out of its sight
For a minute.
Always copying you.
Shadows creeping up on you in the dark.

Steven Laity (9)
St Andrew's CE Primary School, Buckland Monachorum

APPROACHING THE DAY

The bird is like a duck.
It is a crow we hear.
We hear a woodpecker pecking away.
We hear a helicopter *brrruming* away.
We are off to the river.
We can hear Concorde.
I hear a plane.

I see a bird,
Horses, horses! Walking along
the moors.

We are off to the river
but we are not yet there
I hear a jet
zooming by like a
Jumbo jet.
I hear the river floating
away
The river sounds like an aeroplane
I can hear the river clear
I can see a heron
I can feel the wind.

Ross Bratchley (8)
St Andrew's CE Primary School, Buckland Monachorum

MARS

Mars is mighty.
Mars is strong.
Mars is brave.
Mars is big.
Mars is like a
fire shooting through
the sky.
Mars is a god
The God of War.
Mars is mean.
Mars is a killer.
Crash, bang!
Mars has collided
with the Earth.
Towers fall,
Crash, bang!
People are dead.
Some people are alive.
Some are whining
like wounded dogs
Some are shouting
Some are screaming
I say to myself
'Shall I live or
shall I die?

Jennifer Young (8)
St Andrew's CE Primary School, Buckland Monachorum

MY MUM

Bright Mum always smiling at me.
Gay Mum always very happy.
Helpful Mum dinner is served for me.
Clumsy Mum sometimes drops dishes.
Funny Mum sometimes wears silly hats
Angry Mum will rave and riot.
Silent Mum will lie quiet as quiet.
Busy Mum has got a lot to do.
Clever Mum teaches me my sums.
Healthy Mum eats good foods.
Loving Mum hugs me every day.
Fit Mum keeps up the energy.
My Mum is the one I love best.

Rosie James (7)
St Andrew's CE Primary School, Buckland Monachorum

APPROACHING THE RIVER

I hear the woodpecker chattering like teeth
The crow squawking loud as an alarm clock on the moors today.

As we get closer we hear the wind whooshing like a plane
I hear a faint flowing noise like the wind when it hits trees.

Now we are here, Yippee! It is as dark as soil
As peaceful as night. As exciting as an adventure.
I am glad I'm at the river today.

Simon Crimp (9)
St Andrew's CE Primary School, Buckland Monachorum

DRAGON FIRE

In a dark dark cave,
By a dark dark sea,
Lived a dragon.

Topaz gold scales,
Colossal emerald wings,
Sapphire teeth,
Ancient evil eyes and
Ruby hard tail.

In a dark dark cave,
By a dark dark sea,
That dragon still lives.

Thomas Williams (7)
St Andrew's CE Primary School, Buckland Monachorum

MY MUM

Clumsy Mum smashing plates.
Helpful Mum tidies up.
Good Mum washes up.
Happy Mum losing weight.
Cross Mum telling me off.
Calm Mum calming me.
Forgetful Mum forgetting.
Helpful Mum helping me into bed.
Loving Mum loving me.
Kind Mum cuddling me.
Good Mum reading to me.

Joe Ward (7)
St Andrew's CE Primary School, Buckland Monachorum

DRAGON DANGER

This is a dragon with deadly teeth,
sharp claws, blood-red eyes,
even a tail as a whip.
Scary scales,
but there is only one thing
that makes him scary.
He breathes fire!

Ross Symons (8)
St Andrew's CE Primary School, Buckland Monachorum

DRAGON

I met a dragon.
No ordinary dragon.
It was scaly fiery bright huge,
with golden scales gleaming.
This dragon is greedy
and a burglar.
It could set a house on fire.

Lawrence Barnes (8)
St Andrew's CE Primary School, Buckland Monachorum

DEADLY DRAGON

A dragon like a flying lizard.
Eyes like fireballs.
Wings like leather,
With deadly claws.
Sharp teeth like nails
With fiery breath.
He collects gold.

Russell Floyd (8)
St Andrew's CE Primary School, Buckland Monachorum

DOWN IN THE DARK

Down in the dark of the deepest cave,
the last of the giants
and the first of the lizards
is sleeping.
Lying like a large piece of metal
hardly moving,
guarding its gold,
keeping its eye on the huge archway,
watching the glimmer of light,
But nothing happens.

James Lear (8)
St Andrew's CE Primary School, Buckland Monachorum

DRAGON!

Slimy sticky wings.
Sharp spikes.
Blazing hot fire.
Slimy sharp teeth.
Smelly green feet.
Sharp claws.
Lizard-like body.
The scariest monster of them all!

Gary Curtis (8)
St Andrew's CE Primary School, Buckland Monachorum

DRAGON!

In a dank, dark gloomy cave
I saw a dragon.
Smoky hot, fiery nose,
green slimy tongue,
webbed slapping feet,
a fork-like tail,
leathery black wings
boiling bubbling mouth.

Alexander McCormick (8)
St Andrew's CE Primary School, Buckland Monachorum

DRAGON!

A dragon curled up in his mountain lair.
His yellow teeth crashed together.
His rolling eyes glared.
His sharp pointed tail
crashed against the rocks
and his webbed feet battered on the floor,
as he curled around his treasure.

Hannah Moore (8)
St Andrew's CE Primary School, Buckland Monachorum

MY MUM

Happy Mum plays with me.
Angry Mum tells me off.
Tidy Mum keeps the house tidy.
Clumsy Mum drops things.
I love my Mum and she loves me.

Lewis Belcher (6)
St Andrew's CE Primary School, Buckland Monachorum

DRAGON DREAM

I saw the dragon
in my dream.
It was slimy, scaly,
disgusting, fiery,
scary, large eyes,
loud, silly,
greedy meat-eater,
smelly, secret.
I can still see it.

Cecelia Smith (8)
St Andrew's CE Primary School, Buckland Monachorum

THE SLEEPY DRAGON

There was a lazy dragon
who did nothing at all.
All he did was sleep.
He was like a fiery lizard.
He had scales like shimmering metal.
Wings like shimmering birds.
A tail like a hard hammer
and eyes that hypnotise.
A dragon that snores.

Tamsin Bennett (8)
St Andrew's CE Primary School, Buckland Monachorum

DRAGON EYES

When I saw the dragon
he had green vicious eyes
a hot red mouth
armour scales
dagger teeth
a snake-like tail
wings like a blanket of night.

Jamie Henderson (8)
St Andrew's CE Primary School, Buckland Monachorum

MY PET

My pet is golden and greedy,
like a lizard.
His feet are webbed.
He breathes fire.
His eyes are small.
He is cute.
He is tiny
and he's a . . .
Dragon!

Jessica Edy (7)
St Andrew's CE Primary School, Buckland Monachorum

THE ROBE'S DREAM

I remember a long time ago
I was made from fine cotton.
I was large and beautiful
fit for a king.

I am older now.
the King on the cross wore me.
I was taken by soldiers
who played dice for me.
I felt sad to leave my King.

Sarah Greatrex (8)
St Andrew's CE Primary School, Buckland Monachorum

FIREWORKS

Sparklers crackle like
sudden bangs of stars at night.
Roman candles like
the shooting stars in the sky.
Bonfires like flaming dragons breathing.
Catherine wheels like Speedy
Whizzing flowers spinning
round and round.

Elizabeth Wimble (8)
St Andrew's CE Primary School, Buckland Monachorum

GIANT WORLD

Giant world round and wide
Ships sailing round and round,
Pink fish, orange fish
All being caught.
All ducks swimming in blue sea,
Ducks quacking as they swim along.
Dolphins jumping over the rocks.
Swim underwater cry and die.
Sea horses swim around,
Why do all fish like to cry.
I don't know, ask me why
I really want to cry.
Why did I cry?
Because I loved the dolphin
but it cried and died.

Kayleigh Rickards (9)
St George's Primary School, Stonehouse

PRICKLY PLANT

Green prickly living plant with spots soft and
spongy, water and light, it needs lots
Star-shaped and pretty with teeth everywhere.
It lives in soil in a pot and needs lots of care.

Mark Nathan (9)
St George's Primary School, Stonehouse

A BLOWY NIGHT AND A BRIGHT MORNING

I go to bed at 7.30pm
and fall asleep a few hours later
The wind starts to howl
so hard it nearly blows
the cat flap off.
I try to stay asleep
but it gets stronger.
It's like a current.
I hear doors clang.
I shut my eyes and fall asleep.
Morning appears.
I wake up.
I hear the birds sing
I go down to breakfast.
What a night I had.

Adam Voisey (9)
Sandford School

THE CONSTANT HICCUPS

I hate *hicc....ups!*
Hicc....ups are bor....ing.
Hicc....ups stop you from tal...
king in sent....ences.
Hicc....ups hate me.

　　　Hiccups!

Nathan North (9)
Sandford School

I WISH I COULD HELP MORE

I wish I could help more.
I can't bear to just walk past and do nothing.
It just makes me think how lucky we are.
When we're hungry, thirsty or cold we get what
we want.
But they don't.

My family and I give money sometimes.
Big Issue sellers, we buy the magazines if we're in,
say, Exeter or London or some place like that.
They need a bed, a warm place, some food, drink,
care and most of all, hope for the future.
I'm sorry they have to be that way.

Homeless!

Daisy Manson (9)
Sandford School

THE BIG MATCH

He shoots, he scores!
Number nine up the line.
He shoots, heads, he scores.
He shoots, the ball swerves, it hits a man,
The crowd laugh.

It's a good kick!
Number six has the ball and slips.
The crowd laughs again.
Number two kicks, knocks out the goalie.
Shoots again, hits the crossbar, hits the goalie
and goes in, the crowd laughs again!

William O'Sullivan (9)
Sandford School

MY HOME

The cat awakes from his slumber
curls up
and drifts off again.
The fire sizzles as Mum loads on more coal.
Daniel's music booms through the
ceiling as he
sings the prodigy song.
The wind howls round
the chimney pots.
Sizzles as the dinner cooks in the kitchen.

Next door's phone, no answer they have gone to
skittles again.
Dinner's ready.
Yum, yum, chicken burgers and chips.
After dinner I go in a race with
Daniel
to see who gets to their bedroom first.
I win, after all my congratulations
I go in my room.
I hear his computer beating. The beat, stuck in my
head, I go to sleep.

Bethan Lewis (8)
Sandford School

MY DADDY IN THE MORNING

His hair is almost always standing up on end,
His mouth is overflowing with bits of gooey phlegm,
Out of his ears are hanging old bits of cotton wool,
And also out of his mouth splodges slimy bits of drool.
He has for his breakfast, muesli,
Muesli and crumbly toast,
But not from the packet, no, not from the packet,
nor from the crumbly loaf,
Oh really and truly,
Yes really and truly, I think he's a bit of an oaf.
His name is Fred,
Freddie the Dread.
Freddie the dready wed-ned!
He holds in his hands some African sands,
Fine African sands from Kenya.
His beard is big,
Bushy and big,
The home of a tree of a fig,
But that is not all, no that is not all, for plenty of birds
make their nests in his chest
His chest, his chest, his hairy chest!

Isabel Ehresmann (9)
Sandford School

WHY? OR POLLUTION

As the murky sewage flows out of pulsing pipes
and mixes with the dirty river I think why are we
polluting our world?

Why?
Why?
Why are we polluting?
Why?
Why?
Why do we pollute?

As I try to cross the mucky rubbish dump
I think why are we polluting our world?

Why?
Why?
Why do we do this?
Why?
Why?
Why?

War pollutes our happiness let alone our hearts

Why?
Why?
Why is the question
Why?
Why?
Why?

Why do we pollute our world?
Why I ask you, why?

Simply why?

Jason Hunt (9)
Sandford School

CRAZY

'I'm bored,'
'Are you?'
'Yea . . .
So,'
'Shut up!'
'No, I won't,'
'Yes.'
'Don't say that to me!'
'Tough,'
'You be quiet!'
'Pealer,'
'Shut up!'
'Are you starting then?'
'Yea, come on!'
'Try and hit me!'
'OK,'
'Bump,'
'Ahhh!'
'He hurt me,'
'Be quiet!'

Jamie Houlston (9)
Sandford School

ACID RAIN

Acid rain falls down on the ground like chewing gum.
It goes through umbrellas like bolts from the sky.
Smoke from factories makes it worse.
Statues have just been built,
Acid comes down like firing jets and washes them away.
Buildings get washed away to the bottom of its path.

Jamie Fleming (9)
Sandford School

THE BUTTERFLY

The sun curled into the afternoon
Light
And the butterfly flew to
The flower.
She sparkled with delight
As the bee came to join her.
It was quiet and peaceful.
The butterfly gleamed
As on her wing
The pink blended in
And the blue blended back
She blushed like a ball of
Red red colour
Until
The night emerged from the
Depths of the clouds
And the sky became
Duller.
The mist covered over the green
Grass
And the dew began to glisten.
The butterfly lay there
Dead on the ground
As the blue blended in quietly.

Caragh Campbell (8)
Sandford School

MY MAGIC BOX

In my box I have,
A zebra and a cat and much more like that,
A sharp smooth snow leopard that is cool
and waterproof.
A parrot with feathers that shimmer in
the waves of sunlight that spread itself
on the parrot's soft wings;
and the biggest giraffe you have ever seen,
But down near the sea,
There is a very long serpent. With one gulp
you shall go where a secret sunflower grows,
Then down a tube there is a place,
Where I and my best friend go,
to a rainbow of colours, a stream of gold
and a sky of blue velvet,
Once I told my class about my magic box
but no one believed me about the . . .

Zebra,
The cat,
The snow leopard,
The parrot,
The giraffe,
Or the serpent,
But I shall keep it to myself and make sure
that the key doesn't get thrown away.

Laura Smith (9)
Sandford School

WINTER AND SCHOOL DON'T MIX

I am lying in my warm warm bed
it is cosy,
My mum walks in and shouts
'Time for school!'
My ears feel like they're on fire.
I get up and get dressed.
I walk to the door, I open it suddenly
I can feel the cold, cold breeze passing
through my hands and making my body
freeze so I feel like I am going to crack
in half.
I can hear wind swirling round the trees and
pushing into the plants and the birds
Shouting for help.

Finbar Roth (8)
Sandford School

PETS

I have two guinea pigs
One cat and one hamster.
I thought I should call one Toffee because
it is the colour of it.
The other is called Snowy
because it is white.
I do really hate the dirty jobs
like cleaning them out,
getting up in the morning to feed them.
It is very boring,
It is very tiring.
I wish I didn't have them,
I really, really do.

Emma Waterworth (8)
Sandford School

GLOBAL WARMING

Global warming is not what it seems
You may think it's warming you
but really it's warning you.
It's all the pollution,
Car fumes and all.

As I walk through the city
The noise and the smell
I suddenly realise,
It's halfway to hell!

I give a sigh
And wonder why
Why are we polluting?
Why?
Why?
Why?

Christopher Merrett (9)
Sandford School

THE WORLD'S ENVIRONMENT

The world could be so beautiful,
Creatures coming, also going,
People poaching, cutting off the horns,
With a knife.
Now they have no life.
Lovely marine life is wrecked
By submarines.
Population turns into pollution.
Big stains on the manatee's back.

Dominic Pain (9)
Sandford School

REMEMBER THE MESSAGE 'PROTECT'

Help.
Silently echoes through life.
Remember what we are destroying.
Remember
the open world
of
losing green.

Listen to the whispers from
midnight stars.
Listen to the silky trees sway.
Protect this growing life,
A treasure we do not see or keep
in our hearts.
The human race, powerful, selfish
mammals
Murderers destroying kindness
Danger creeps over, won't stop.
Listen to the needed
Message,
Help and
Protect!

Ruby Grantham (9)
Sandford School

GOING TO THE HAIRDRESSER'S WITH MY DAD

She or he ask you do you want
a cup of tea.
I say, 'Yes, certainly
of course.'
Off she or he goes.
They fetch a cup of tea,
I take a sip,
then snip, snip, snip!
The hair goes into the cup of tea.
I put it down
and don't say a word.
Then - she cuts the back!
Itch, itch, itch,
Scratch, scratch, scratch,
Out we go, I say 'Phew!
I'm glad that is over,
I am stiff from scratching, Dad.'
'Oh dear, Son,
had a bad
haircut?'

Yann Frampton (9)
Sandford School

MJASBBIIBTTNTIIBFSB

Miss Newman said
Jasz's table I'm watching you
And it's like watching a load of
Slugs working.
But then Jack . . .
But I couldn't hear
I was day-dreaming.
I was in a fish tank
But not an ordinary fish tank.
There was a school of fish -
That's a school of fish
Not a shoal of fish -
Two minutes later
I was out of the dream.
I nearly got told off
But I said it was
Finbar's day-dream powder
So I didn't
But somebody else did.

Jack Honeysett (9)
Sandford School

HOW I HATE MY SISTER]

How I hate my sister, she's really
dumb, she argues with our
mum but then
Mum smacks my bum.
She blames it
all on me then she tells me off
and then my sister comes along and chases me
up a tree.

Scott Mills (8)
Sandford School

GET YOUR OWN BACK SHOP

A packet of sprinkles to enlarge a bottom!
A bucket of lies, white or black, for an enemy.
A packet of rainbow tears, for the funniest clown.
Some lavender chocolate for breath sweet.
A packet of gobstoppers, to eagerly fine up your rotten teeth.
A packet of wind beans so you can burp, burp, all day.
Some horrendous itching powder for teachers' gym clothes.
A pot of shoe polish that makes you bounce all the time.
Some extra super super glue, to glue your dad's hat.
Some peas to flick your sisters with,
Some special water which makes them quiet.

Emily Pitts (9)
Sandford School

FOOTBALL

Football's a team sport, you're
always on the run.
Chase the ball.
The ref gives a red card.
You get sent off.
Hang your head in shame
In the changing room
lonely tears run down your cheeks.

Goal!

Shouts the commentator!
You rush out of the changing room.
It was the other team.

Daniel Stenson (9)
Sandford School

FROM YOUR ONE TRUE LOVE

As the rain pours
and the sun shines
somewhere a pot of
gold lurks.
I follow colours of
red, orange, yellow,
green, blue, indigo
and violet.
My heart bleeds
not for gold rings,
gold nuggets, gold coins
the gold heart . . .
No!
For the loving gold in you.

Kate Baker (9)
Sandford School

UP IN THE SKY

Up in the sky, where everything moves,
Up in the sky, where the sun moves,
Up in the sky, where the sun moves round the world,
Up in the sky, where the shooting stars are,
Up in the sky, where flying saucers are,
Up in the sky, where the moon is,
Up in the sky, where the spacemen are,
Up in the sky, where aliens live,
Up in the sky, where rockets go,
Up in the sky, where black holes are,
Up in the sky, where the universe is,
Up in the sky, where plants are,
Up in the sky, how I wish I could fly!

Grace Whitton (9)
The Dolphin School

MY NAME IS MR COSMIC

My name is Mr Cosmic,
I am an old magician,
Although my acts go terribly wrong,
I still enjoy doing them.

My name is Mr Cosmic,
I have a show every night,
I made a human disappear,
It wasn't supposed to happen!

My name is Mr Cosmic,
I ride upon a roller-coaster,
I want to go to space,
But I can't stop my magic,
I love it!

My name is Mr Cosmic,
If I do my magic upon the moon,
I'll lose all my equipment,
I shall be a sight to see.

My name is Mr Cosmic,
I would love to live on Mars,
I could eat lots of chocolate,
And then I would get fat.

My name is Mr Cosmic,
I would love to see real aliens,
The planets are like one thousand balls
Rolling down on me.

My name is Mr Cosmic,
I am an old magician,
Although my acts go terribly wrong,
I still enjoy doing them.

Amanda Fowler (8)
The Dolphin School

A MISS DELAY

I was flying in an aeroplane,
That went a little high,
It turned into a bright blue rocket,
But I don't know why!

We were planning to go to Spain,
But then we went to Space,
I shall lose all my packages,
But I'll bring them just in case!

We wanted a sunny time,
So we went visiting Mercury,
It was hotter than the airing cupboard,
And I lost my cuddly toy!

My younger sister, she's just a menace,
She's lost her toy as well,
That would keep her happy,
But now it sounds like hell!

I've lost my homework too,
My teacher will be mad,
But I do hate my homework,
So I'm rather glad.

I know we'll all be dying soon,
But then it's not our fault,
I wish I was in Spain though,
But I would get back and get taught!

I nearly lost my mother,
But she did float down,
I'm just so glad there's lots together,
It's just like being back in town!

'Space is mad,'
Says Mum and Dad.

Victoria Launchbury (8)
The Dolphin School

MY GARDEN

I saw an alien in my garden,
picking flowers and saying,
'Pardon!' . . . then it disappeared.

I saw a star in my garden,
Eating cheese and picking weeds,
then . . . it disappeared

I saw a planet in my garden,
going round and round. I said 'Stop
that now' and then . . . it disappeared

I saw a spaceman in my garden,
he was big, fat and ugly and then . . .
he disappeared.

But then my teacher appeared
and then disappeared . . .

            in my garden!

Kelly Miller (9)
The Dolphin School

It's Only a Dream!

Tonight it is a full moon,
I look out my window,
And there I see in front of me two red eyes,
Coming from a grey racoon.

Wolves are howling under the stars,
The wonders of the darkness glooming,
And if you look up high you would be able
To see Mars.

There it is in front of my bed,
Staring into my eyes.
'I can't see over your head,' I said!
'Agghh!'

Now it's right in front of me,
All around my bed, there they are, all of them,
Please don't make it true,
It can't be.

I finally recovered from all the stress,
Once again I went to my window,
And looked down at my garden shed.
There it stood.

A big, slimy, green monster,
Camouflaged into the grass.
Am I having another nightmare?
I think I'll just have to pass!

'Oh no!'

On second thoughts, I think I'll go back to bed!
On third thoughts, I might run away and go.
No!

Thank goodness for that, it's only a dream!
Next time, I'll know to scream!

Tabitha Lucy Quilter (9)
The Dolphin School

A TRIP IN SPACE!

I was walking along on the moon,
When I heard something of a *boom!*
I ran away,
And said, 'Hooray!'
While walking on the moon.

I was zooming round a planet,
And I could hardly stand it,
An alien came out,
And threw me out,
And said, *'Go gle - adit!'*

I was whizzing around in space,
At a very slow pace,
I flew down,
And gave a frown,
When a Martian came down,
And made himself at home in our town.

Ben Hutchings (9)
The Dolphin School

?

What's that out in my
garden? Is it a bird, is
it an alien?
No, it's a fox.

What's that falling through
the air? Is it Super Man,
or is it a meteorite?
No, it's an aeroplane.

What's that in the
bush? Is it a cat,
or is it tiny spacemen?
No, it's a badger.

What's that going across the
moon? Is it a rocket, or
is it a flying saucer?
No, it's Father Christmas.

What's that going across
my bed? It's slimy!
It's licking me!
Phew! It's only my dog!

What's going across
my floor? Is it a
snake, or is it a little alien?
No, it's a spider.

What's going up into the
sky? It's a plane, isn't it?
But it hasn't got wings.
It has got to be a plane.
It has got to be . . .

Aghaaghaa!

Alice Bowring (9)
The Dolphin School

IN SPACE

I was flying through space,
When an alien went in my face!
We made friends,
Went round some tight bends,
He helped me but kept saying *'Bibwace!'*
Then I came across ET,
He was a member of BT.
He wanted to phone home,
So I gave him a phone,
And then had lunch that was meaty.
Then I went back into space,
I found an alien in my parking place,
I finally found a base,
And stayed at the Hotel Mace.

Mark Massarik (9)
The Dolphin School

MY POTION

Ogle boggle
An eye and an ear,
Drop some blood in
And make it clear.

Some guts of a slug,
And maybe some bugs,
Crunch them up till
They all disappear.

And last of all,
To sum it up,
Some beetles' blood.
Go bubble bubble pop!

Give it to your gran
Loopy lops she goes
Bright red she will turn
And bananas she will go.

Kylie Rowe (9)
Uplowman Primary School

FLY AWAY, FLY AWAY!

Fly away, fly away,
Over the sea,
Sun-loving swallow,
For summer is done.

Come again, come again,
Come back to me,
Bringing the summer and
Bringing the sun.

Celia Hodgson (7)
Uplowman Primary School

ONE MORE STEP ALONG THE WORLD I GO

One more step along the world I go.
Sorry Christopher I did not know.
Hamish and Michael stop licking your toes.
And James stop picking your nose.

> *Chorus*
>
> *And it's from the old I travel to the new,*
> *Keeping me travelling without you.*

Round the corner of the world I go
More and more you have to be told.

As I travel through the bad and good
Keep me safe and do the things I should.

Colin Nicholls (8)
Uplowman Primary School

THE MAN FROM BRISTOL

There once was an old man from Bristol
Who had a little toy pistol
He did something too
Just like you
That silly old man was from Bristol.

Tim Sheridan (8)
Uplowman Primary School

THE OLD MAN

There was once an old man
He owned a very old van
But one day it got hit with a pan
That poor old van.

He went to get another
But they were all covered in leather
He told the shopkeeper Trevor
He didn't like them covered in leather.

The shopkeeper said 'They're the only
ones we've got
You either take one or read Esio Trot
You can tell we've got a lot
So take one or you will be in a giant cot.

Kieran Knowles (8)
Uplowman Primary School

THERE WAS A MAN

There was a man
Who had an illuminous van
He loved it very much.
He goes to other countries
Eating lots of Munchies
It is great fun.
He enjoys it very much
Pulling the clutch
He finds it great fun.

Mark Ede (9)
Uplowman Primary School

THE FLYING PIG

The flying pig in the air.
Going so fast, so fast.
In the air all of the time.
All of the people under him were amazed.
Over the hills and the farms.
Over everything.
The pig has come down.
Get him get him from behind the tree.
He is going down the river.
Splash! He is in the river.
He is a swimming pig now.

Simon Hawkins (8)
Uplowman Primary School

CLOUDS

It looks soft, puffy and cuddly.
It makes me feel hot and nice.
Appears to look like a soft bed.

It is like horrible and wet.
Makes me feel sad.
A chain of water.

It is like a hurried drawing.
Makes me feel like a good girl
Rushing on a motorway.

Tracey Hutchings (8)
Winkleigh CP School

CLOUDS

The clouds look like ice-cream.
Big and bushy and plump.
They make me feel joyful,
And good inside.

Streaky string across the sky.
It makes me feel like running.
The sun will shine
And it makes me do cartwheels.

Makes me feel rough and mad.
The clouds look like mud.
They get big bobbly and fat.
They make me frightened and scared.
Goes black and it is cool.

Sally Rogers (9)
Winkleigh CP School

THE WIND

It feels cold, bitter and freezing
It tastes nice, funny and bitter
It sounds funny and horrible
It looks see-through and windy
It smells like nothing
The wind feels like a big quilt
The wind tastes like melted ice-cream
It sounds like someone whistling
It looks like a ghost
It smells like a cow-pat
I can imagine the wind making people cold.

Lucy Adkins (8)
Winkleigh CP School

THE CLOUDS

White fluffy clouds look like polar bears
Dancing in the sky.
Make me happy, look like ice.
And sort of look like white fluffy mice.
Black clouds clumped together
Making a sort of picture of night.
Shadows filling up the sky
That makes me want to die.
Twirling around making a whirlwind
They make sure that they are spread around.
Make me feel kind and happy.
Black clouds make me feel sad, frightened.
Unhappy, dark inside.
Thin, creepy clouds make me feel quite happy.

Hannah McGregor (9)
Winkleigh CP School

CLOUD

It looks really really fluffy
It makes me very happy
I imagine it is very soft
To me it looks like candyfloss.

It looks very very angry
It makes me really sad
To me it is a beetle
It is very very thin.
It makes me feel alright
To me it looks like ice.

Ashley James McGinley (9)
Winkleigh CP School

THE FRIENDLY CLOUD

Hot
Joyful
Cuddly like a fluffy white kitten

Nice
Friendly
Caring when I look up to the sky above.

The clouds are a friend to me

The clouds are nice and friendly
Caring and very joyful to me.

Kylie Bridgman (9)
Winkleigh CP School

CLOUDS

They are fluffy.
I feel happy
The clouds are pillows for angels.

They are stormy and black
I feel sad
The clouds are the sea
Boats sailing, sinking.

They are cats' whiskers and licks
I feel happy and sad
The cats' whiskers
Are pretty.

Claire Symonds (9)
Winkleigh CP School

THE WIND

On a hot summer's day the wind feels cool,
On a cold winter's day the wind blows shrill,
Feel it on your face, it's quite a chill.
Down by the beach it tastes like the sea, so salty.
Imagine the wind as a wild animal
roaring and barking And chasing the birds.
Or as gentle as clouds Floating up there.
In cities the wind smells musty.
In the country it just smells dusty.
The wind feels so gentle blowing through my hair.
In winter the wind sounds like a bear.
In the summer it sounds like the leaves
rustling in the trees.

Jamie Short (9)
Winkleigh CP School

CLOUDS

It looks all bushy
It looks like candyfloss
I look at them
They make me feel good.

Is very powerful
It looks like ashes from a fire.
Scared feelings inside.

Looks like a tractor
Going in the sky
Like a paintbrush
Going right on
I feel like painting now.

James Popham (8)
Winkleigh CP School

THE CLOUDS

Stormy rain-clouds
Black as night
On some days
You can see a golden rim
Around the edge of the clouds
Like over a tropical island
The clouds are now racing over the sky
They are like racehorses going round and
Round and round
No clouds in the sky
Blue sky raging sun
But now the clouds are
Coming back
The sun has gone
Here come the black clouds
To cover the sky in black
People go indoors, shut the windows
It's going to rain.

Stephen Hill (9)
Winkleigh CP School

THE WIND

See. I can see wind blowing down
roofs blowing down houses and leaves all around.

Smell. Wind smells horrible, blocks up my
nose, does things horrible to my hands.

Feel. Wind feels gentle on my hands and
on my face.

Hear. Wind sounds solid to my ears,
makes windows rattle.

Taste. Wind tastes fresh, makes my mouth dry.

Imagine. I imagine wind will blow and blow.

Gemma Anstey (8)
Winkleigh CP School

THE FLUFFY CLOUDS

Clouds are like a cotton ball,
Clouds are hot and sometimes cool,
They are fluffy, feathery, low and high
And when you see the black clouds
People always sigh.
There are cloud men up in the sky,
They are really, really high,
Digging and working,
Wondering and lurking around.
When it is snowing,
It is really the cloud men throwing
Down bits of cloud.
Clouds are wet
But when the sun sets
They look pink and orange.
Clouds are like a cotton ball,
Clouds are hot and sometimes cool.

Liesa Down (9)
Winkleigh CP School

CLOUD

It looks puffy
I feel hot
Soft and fluffy
Summery feelings
It wants me to lie down.

        It's nasty and black
        I am cold
        Frightened and scared
        Stormy tornadoes coming
        Horrible weather.

Wavy ribbons
Floating by a man
Picking up snow
I feel brilliant inside.

Rebecca Roberts (8)
Winkleigh CP School

CLOUDS

When I look at the sky
It makes me happy
There are fluffy clouds
Candyfloss shapes.

        Looks black like night
        I feel frightened they might fall
        Tornadoes going over the sky.

There are paintbrushes
On the sky that make
Lines across the clouds.

Sophie Popham (8)
Winkleigh CP School